Basics and Benefits of Composting

By David Brian

Basics and Benefits of Composting

David Brian

Administrator of RedWormFarms.com

Basics and Benefits of Composting
Copyright 2020 by David Brian

Publisher: BN Publishing

ISBN 978-8272359941

Table of Contents

OTHER BOOKS BY DAVID BRIAN

Basics and Benefits of Worm Composting

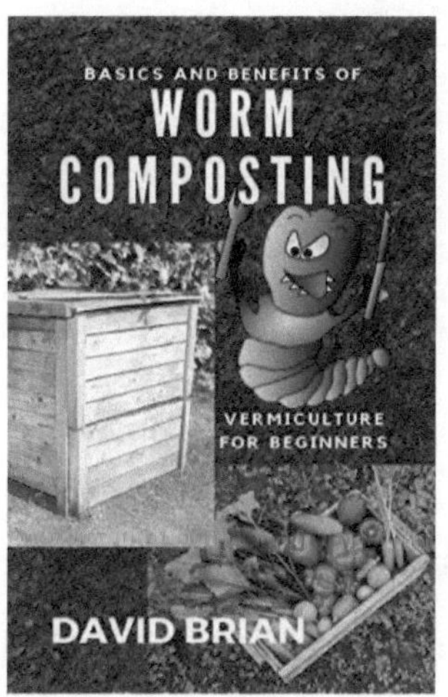

Welding Tipps and Tricks

FOREWORD

9

For many years I have been administering my website RedWormFarms.com and I very much like writing an article for my site from time to time. I enjoy writing about my "Babies" - the red worms or red wigglers.

However, in this small book I would like to talk about composting in general: Why and how to start, what to consider, how to choose, etc.

Naturally, I also included a small part on worm composting.

David Brian, December 2020

WHY SHALL I COMPOST?
7 TOP REASONS FOR COMPOSTING

Until today you might have been hesitant in making and using compost. You find the task of making one troublesome and time consuming. Or you might have false perceptions of smelly compost piles and having such a messy process right in your backyards. While others would prefer buying their fertilizers, soil amendments or conditioners, and mulch from their garden stores to avoid all the hassle of reading about compost and actually making one.

But you have bought this book, so you are interested.

Here are my top personal reasons for composting. I hope I am able to convince you and you begin your own compost pile before you reach reason number seven.

NUMBER ONE: IT'S FREE!

The first reason I find composting highly worthwhile is the fact that the materials used are absolutely free and are readily available. Compare that with the ever rising costs of commercial fertilizers and other gardening products in the market today. All you need is a little extra effort to find the best materials for your compost pile, but otherwise, everything's for free.

Number Two: More Nutrients & Minerals

The second one is that compost provides more nutrients and minerals needed by my plants than commercial organic or synthetic fertilizers. The overall effect of compost is also longer than commercially available fertilizers. It's free and it works better, who wouldn't want that? Plus, if you organize your ingredients just right, you can provide a whole lot more range of nutrients.

Number Three: Good for the Soil

Another good reason would be the benefits of compost to the soil structure. When applied to the soil, compost can help the soil be more resistant to erosion, improve its retention of water, and in some types of soil (like clay) it can reduce the chance the soil becomes compact. This is also important for farmers since compost can make the soil easier to till conserving time and fuel needed to operate the machines.

Number Four: Kill the Weeds

With the right composting technique, the process can kill those troublesome weeds as well as pests and disease-causing organisms present in the materials being composted. High temperature composting is the technique I am talking about. Although, this technique is not the backyard variety but rather a more laboratory or industrial type variety, I still find it a good reason why we should make composts.

NUMBER FIVE: RESIST DISEASES, PEST & INSECTS

There have been studies which indicate that using compost can suppress the growth of diseases in crops. Other studies also show that crops grown over compost rich soils can resist better pest or insect attacks. Likewise, some news and observations in the field also shows that crops grown using compost bear produce that can be stored longer. If that's not reason enough, I don't know what else you are looking for.

NUMBER SIX: REDUCE CARBON DIOXIDE

For the environmentalists and conservationists, compost has something for them as well. Using compost together with the soil can build soil carbon which can eventually reduce the carbon dioxide in the atmosphere. It may take a lot of compost to have a positive effect on the greenhouse gases but that fact is quite useful as well.

NUMBER SEVEN: REDUCE TOXICS

It is also found out that compost works well as an antidote for soils that are toxic with agricultural chemicals. Compost can balance the levels of soil acidity, and helps farmers to go organic after years of using synthetic agricultural products.

These are my top reason for composting. Some of it may not directly benefit your personal needs but having those reasons to cling onto is a good thing to motivate the use of compost.

Introduction and Quick Start to Composting

If you care about the environment, you will be in favor of the composting process. This concept is all about giving back to the land what it has given you. It is all about recycling. It is all about a cycle that things go through in order to grow.

It is an interesting cycle. If you just take a moment to take a deeper look into a pile of decaying things, you will see that some things that are slowly becoming part of the land. And you also see some offspring that are growing from the process.

That's life. And that's how your life is also going to be. If you are in touch with nature, you will see such cycles as miracles, and something to be joyful about.

Compost is also more than just a using fertilizer on soil. This actually means that the cycle of life goes on. You can gather decaying leaves of plants and other manures and things that can be found in your garden for this purpose. You will then use all the materials to form your very own compost.

This process is actually practiced by many farmers in all parts of the world. But ordinary gardeners or people who love nature and things that revolve in it can also benefit from this.

The organic residue that you collect when you gather different materials from the land that is converted into something black, somewhat fragrant, and crumbly (decomposing) is what will be the compost. The idea here is to arrange the materials so that the soil bacteria and fungi can survive and also multiply as they all break down. The bacteria act as the converters of all raw materials so that they must be in a workable environment with proper moisture, food and air.

If you haven't made yours, but are interested in starting a compost, you can begin by gathering the green and dry elements that you can see around your garden. You must think what you can feed the bacteria for it to thrive. For such, you can tap on the grass clippings, the green weeds, as well as the vines of pea and leaves of lettuce. What do they have in common? They contain sugar elements as well as proteins and they all can decompose fast.

Dry leaves and other small twigs must be mixed with the greens when decomposing. These materials take a lot of time in order to decompose because they contain little nitrogen. That is why they must not be left alone in the process.

You can also build a compost pile by mixing a fertilizer, then adding manure and garden soil between every layer of your gathered waste material.

You need not be a pro to be able to come up with your own version of this tool. All you've got to have is a big heart for nature and you are set to go.

What you have to remember is that you are doing the environment a great favor by being involved in such a process. Not everyone loves to garden, having said that, it is also true that not everyone will love the idea of making compost.

Practice will make everything perfect. This is also true with the idea of composting. Through time, you will be able to develop your own techniques. And hopefully, you will be able to share with others what a gem you have found in this kind of process.

Garden Composter - How to Choose?

How do you choose which type of garden composter to use? There are so many ways of doing garden composting and so many different types of garden compost bins. The choice is obviously a very personal one, dictated by budget, style, and how quickly you hope to make garden compost. To help you decide which option to go for, we'll look at those you can buy and those that are free. To get started lets you take a look at the most commonly used garden compost bin styles available for purchase.

Enclosed Compost Bins for Static Garden

These are compact garden composters that keep out vermin and rain whilst keeping warm. Those tend to be the cheapest types of garden compost bin bought, and the most favored by those new to garden composting. They keep it tidy and safe. You can choose from the wooden composter beehive or the cheaper plastic compost bins. Make sure your compost has ventilation holes to allow oxygen in. Ideally go for a model which has an opening at the base to allow the finished product to be easily removed. Garden composters are readily available made of 100 per cent recycled plastic so don't worry too much about the environmental impact of buying a plastic model.

The downside with included bins is that turning the compost can be difficult, unless you have a very strong friend to help separate the bin from the compost itself. On the plus side it's relatively fast because they keep the garden waste warm and moist composting and you should have created some rich compost even without turning. These sealed garden compost bins should generally give you compost of good quality within six months. Using these in particularly cold regions or where there is a very small amount of garden waste and kitchen scraps could mean that the compost will take up to two years to create. Still, this is the worst case scenario and not a common scenario. A sealed budget plastic compost bin in the UK (not known for fun summers) often produced healthy hummus in under six months.

MOVING COMPOST BINS IN GARDEN

These are a brand new and trendy concept in the typically staid garden composting environment. You can roll the rolling bins to wherever your garden waste is, fill them, then roll them off to wherever you want. Giving them a quick roll every couple of days mixes garden waste and kitchen scraps, allowing for oxygen in and accelerating the decomposition. These keep out vermin and rain, and heat in the same way as the static bins. But they do make the pile very simple to aerate. The downside is that when they're full they get pretty heavy. They are useful if you have plenty of flat space, as you can roll the bin around your garden from project to filling project.

COMPOST TUMBLERS OR COMPOST ROTATING BINS

These plastic garden compost bins come in a host of different styles. All allow the whole bin to be turned onto its axis to mix and aerate the contents. So efficient are these, that they make it much faster than normal to create useful garden compost. Some gardeners say they can use these bins to produce compost within weeks. They'll easily halve the amount of time it takes to create your compost.

Some models come with a collection system to give you compost tea, which is a great concentrated plant food, easily. Several have two chambers that are a great option (funds allowing) because it means that you can always have one compost pile ready to use while another is being created. Be sure to try to avoid those that rotate on their short axis (i.e. those that stand upright) while contemplating a Compost Tumbler. While these are often the cheaper options, and great to start with, they quickly become very heavy to rotate. The ones that are horizontal are much easier to use, rotating on the long axis means it takes far less effort to get them to spin.

These are growing in popularity although more expensive than static compost bins because they produce the finished compost so quickly. With these bins the only real drawback is that they appear to be a little bigger and more expensive than static bins. But, more than does their speed and efficiency make up for that.

WORM MAKERS

Also in popularity vermiculture or worm composting is increasing. Don't miss my site RedWormFarms.com on this topic! Worms very quickly create compost and are happy to consume a wide variety of kitchen scraps to do so. A compact, controlled device like that is suitable for those with limited space. Still, worms need administration. That is not a device that you can overlook. Temperature in particular can be a problem, so it is important to consider where to site a worm farm out of cold drafts, and hot sunlight. Worm Farm Garden Compost Bins are easiest to keep indoors, where fluctuations in temperature are less likely. Properly managed worms will break down your kitchen scraps very quickly and you can easily collect the compost tea they produce once again. So you also get instant liquid plant feed, as well as fast compost.

These are a decent way to recycle kitchen scraps but if you produce a lot of garden waste you'll always need a garden composter. This, however, keeps all the vermin indoors collecting food waste so you can opt for a more accessible (and cheaper) garden compost tank.

COMPOSTERS OPEN TO THE GARDEN

For the sake of fairness I provide these composters with open garden. They're a valid choice. We used open systems to produce wonderful (if slow) compost to the garden. I can't recommend paying for one however. They aren't that expensive but I'm sure you could use wood scraps or wire fencing to do the same. You can get a large plastic compost bin for double the money, and in a fraction of the time create your garden compost. If money is not an option, then they are useful. These are a good way to keep various composting materials tidy and ready to put in a composter for hot greenhouse.

HOW TO SELECT A GARDEN COMPOSTER

Really budget is key in which you choose garden compost bin. There are variations in size but even the smallest garden will contain most varieties of garden composter. A compost tumbler is probably the winner for me just because it works so fast but I have to say that the humble plastic garden compost bin is always a favorite. Over the years they are inexpensive enough to buy a few, and you can have various composting states available. They usually act fairly quickly and last forever.

I think basic is better sometimes, so I'm a fan of the simple plastic garden compost bin, but that's just my point of view. One notice-think about the color. Many of the compost bins in the garden come in a confounding variety of shades of green. Not all will disappear into the view of your backyard. Black, on the other hand it still vanishes into the background. Now you have some details on what your choices are if you are looking to buy a composter for a greenhouse.

How to start Composting in Winter

Your Options

At some time in the year it's time for us to consider how we can compost our kitchen scraps all year round, especially as fall approaches. To many, living in the world's snowy areas makes it at best impossible to think about composting during the winter. However, when having rich fertilizer ready for your gardening efforts next spring, there are a few things you can do to reduce your landfill footprint year round. Here are just a few different winter composting options:

1. ***Indoor compost with worms***
2. ***Composting worms outside***
3. ***Traditional compost approaches outdoor***

Indoor worm composting is, to me, the best solution for the average household. Many citizens, however, have a decent piece of land to deal with, and maybe a lot of land waste itself. To those occasions, both with and without worms can be composted outdoors with a little extra work during the year.

Worms Composting Indoors

Let's look at the first option: Worms composting indoors. The first thing you need to get going is a bin for your worms to be living in. You can create several different types of worm bins using nothing more than a rubbermaid bin and a drill. Many, many bins from producers such as the Can-O-Worms, Gusanito Worm Farm, Wriggly Wranch and others are also on the market. These pre-made bins are intended for use indoors; they are nice to look at, relatively easy to harvest from worm castings, and reasonably priced. Personally, I've got my Gusanito bin in my pantry and my worms look awfully healthy. If you choose to build your own indoor worm bin, then this is a simple way to do it. Choose an opaque rubber maid or similar bin; worms don't like the light, and don't like a see-through bin. Drill many holes for drainage along your bin's rim. Using the bin's lid to store any excess liquid. Use small wood blocks or something similar to let the bin rest just one or two inches above the lid; this allows any extra fluid to flow easily out of the bin and into the lid. A worm bin is composed of both bedding materials and worm food materials. After a lot of experimentation I found coconut coir or peat moss to be the best materials to be used as bedding. These materials provide good airflow while at the same time helping to keep flies out, so they are my preference. You can also use shredded paper but I suggest that it be finely shredded before use to help deter pests as well.

So, it's time to make a worm lasagna now that you've got your bin. You're going to add a few inches of moist bedding, dump in a nice pile in your worms, add another inch of moist bedding, add your kitchen scraps, then add two or three more inches of moist bedding. I like the method of lasagna as it facilitates the upward migration of worms to food and helps you to literally lay more food as you go. Sprinkle ground cinnamon generously on top of your top bedding sheet. Cinnamon is a natural insecticide, and will not appeal to flies. This bin I just mentioned is an open device, or a container without a lid. I've found that keeping worms where they belong is simpler if your bins don't have lids. Worm bins with lids also cause condensation along the walls of the interior, which means roaming worms. Even a bin with a lid would provide even less ventilation for your little buddies and they do need to breathe!

Keep a small receptacle near the sink for everyday use, to collect food for your worms. Then, having a larger receptacle in your freezer is wise; this will keep flies away and also help break down the worm food when it thaws. Then, toss the whole contents onto your bin's top layer weekly, and layer again with 3-4 inches of dry bedding. You can thaw the kitchen scraps on the counter and then mix them in a blender or cuisinart if you want to reduce the possibility of flies any further. That makes the waste both easier for the worms to eat faster, and it's also hard for flies to find a nice sticky place to lay their eggs. A well tended washbasin will not be stinky. If you get some unpleasant odors it means you overfed the worms and they cannot keep up. Stop feeding until the smells go away, and it's clear that the worms on the scraps they already have are making good headway.

WORMS COMPOSTING OUTDOORS

Now let's talk about composting worms outdoors. Thinking that worms can survive an outdoor arctic-like winter may seem insane, but they can certainly do if you give them what they need: warmth and food. First you need to find a place on your property where you'll create a pile of worm compost. You will need to find a good number of straw or hay bales to build the walls of your system after you take a rough measurement (try craigs list). Place them in twos around the edge of your planned worm bed. Then it is time another worm lasagna was made. Start with carton on the ground to serve as a false backdrop to your "pot." And continue to attach layers of yard clippings, leaves, scraps of food and manure. Manure is the main ingredient in a winter worm bed outside, since it produces a lot of heat as it decomposes. Once again, search the craigslist for horse or cow barns in the garden section where you can openly go upload. When the bed is set up, add the worms to it. Drape a black tarp over the entire lot until they have dived deep into the products. The tarp will retain both moisture and gather heat from the sun when it appears in the winter months. If you decide to try a worm bed in winter make sure you have enough worms to process the materials. A good thumb rule is 1 pound per square foot of surface area (though you might get away with less than that). You must also be committed to checking on your worms regularly. Buy a compost thermometer or remote sensor thermometer to make sure the worm bed temperature is about 55-77 degrees Fahrenheit. You can follow the same concept as with composting indoor worms and store your food scraps in the freezer. Then take away the container weekly outside and bury the contents in the existing worm bedding.

There's one special commercial outdoor worm bin for wintertime that I've seen and I have to admit it's fascinating. It is called the Wigwam Worm. This unit is a flow-through system that enables castings to be harvested from the bottom, and it also has a heater that makes it ideal for composting winter worms outdoors. Unfortunately at around $600 it's pretty expensive. If you don't find the cost prohibitive, then give this unit a try anyway.

Winter Composting without Worms

Winter outdoor composting without worms can work in much the same way as worms do. You can build the same kind of insulated pile, and be sure to add plenty of manure to heat generation. The only difference is that you will regularly aerate the pile (whereas worms naturally do this). That means you'll need to get bundled up and go out with your shovel at least weekly to manually transform the contents of your pile. Oxygen is required in the decomposition process, so if you want to use this form of pile this is a must-do.

Early Preparation

For any form of composting method, you must plan during the summer / fall to be effective in the winter. Before temperature drops too far, make sure you get your system installed and up and running. Otherwise you may be tempted to just stay in your jammies all winter until spring and forget about the whole composting thing. Yet becoming green is an affair that lasts a year, so be prepared in advance so you can continue to do your part for the environment and produce the organic fertilizer you will need for next year.

COMPOSTING - OTHER FORMS

"PASSIVE" COMPOSTING

If you fall into the category of people who simply do not have the time, space or amount of compostable material to maintain a compost pile or container, you will find some alternatives. These all fall under a passive composting heading since, once the organic waste has been added to the system, they require little further work. Passive composting is the way nature composts, and is sometimes regarded as a lazy manner of composting. Most proponents of passive composting would likely prefer the term smart to lazy. Sheet composting removes the compost pile, as the composting materials are distributed over the ground in layers, typically in a flower or vegetable bed. This is a slow process, but if you're willing to wait, you can sit back with your feet supported and let Mother Nature take her course. As layers decompose, additional layers could be added and the bed depth built up. This approach is perfect for disposing of all fall leaves because many people take the time to rake up and bag for disposal, you may also end up collecting bagged leaves for additional material from some of your neighbors. Since sheet composting lends itself to every form of compostable material, you may leave materials trimmed from your garden lying on the ground and then cover it with leaves and in the spring before this decomposed material gets into the greenhouse.

Why take the time and energy to bring all your cuttings back to the compost pile, only to bring back the finished compost to the garden? Some people go as far as removing their vegetable waste from the property, clearing a spot in the yard, spreading the vegetable waste on the ground and then covering it with a leaf or mulch layer. Stepping on the household waste will continue the material breakdown a little quicker. If you are trying this sheet form, just be aware that this way of composting will attract unwanted creatures to your yard. In addition, sheet composting can be used to create new garden beds without all the usual backbreaking work. All you need is to identify the bed area, then cut everything down to the ground inside that room. Next, cover the cleared area with 8-10-page thick layers of newspapers. Wet the newspapers to help keep them in place and cover them to a depth of at least several inches with mulch or leaves. You can also continue to add materials to the area, such as grass or garden clippings. Depending on where you live, the field will be gone, weeds, roots and everything in 6 months to a year all that grows beforehand. All you left is soil that is rich in organic materials ready to be planted.

ONCE AGAIN – WORM COMPOSTING

Given the worms, worm composting (vermicomposting) is growing in popularity. Worms are the true workhorses in the garden when it comes to transforming organic materials into compost, and even if you don't have a yard you can easily train those guys to work for you. Since worm composting is almost odorless, it can be accomplished in an apartment, but most people prefer a basement or garage.

Worms digest food waste, even peach pits are gone and leave "vermicompost" worm casting behind which is considered to be some of the best compost available. All that is needed to start vermicomposting is the worms and a container to hold the worms and the waste food. If you can't find them nearby, you can order them online. Most can be anything of the container. Holden boxes were originally the containers of choice, now many people use commercially available worm composters. Home made bins can be readily available in large box stores from cheap plastic storage containers. Make sure that the container has 1/4 inch drainage holes in the bottom. Add about 8 inches of suitable bedding fabrics, worms, and scraps of vegetables like potato skins, coffee grounds, moldy bread. The system, once set up, starts to be self-regulating. The worms will start digesting them as the food materials break down and turn them into 'castings.' The more food you have, the more worms it will be made to eat. Cut back on food, and decrease the amount of worms. If you start to notice odors, you are probably overfeeding and need to reduce the amount of food for some time. Just start feeding on one side of the bin, to harvest the compost. All the worms will migrate to the side of the bin which contains the food in about a month, leaving the other half of the bin available for harvest.

Since worm composting is clean, self-contained and nearly odorless, many dwellers in apartments are ardent worm composters. Single people were known to use one gallon of milk containers to compost on their kitchen countertop to produce enough compost to maintain houseplants. The composting trench is exactly what it infers. Dig a trench about a foot deep and start filling it with kitchen or garden organic waste, avoid meat, bones and fatty food. As you fill the trench with rubbish, you cover up as you go. This has the benefit of helping to keep out unwanted creatures. One system that the English developed many years ago and that is particularly well suited for vegetable gardens involves laying out three rows. The first line is for planting, the second row is for walking and the third row is for composting trench. The rows are rotated each year, so that the row used to plant the first year becomes the composting row for the second year and the walking row for the third year. This way, the row used for first year composting will have two years to break down the waste before crops are planted on it.

POST-HOLE COMPOSTING

Post-hole composting is a variation in trench composting, and probably goes back to when man started farming first. Everyone is familiar with the Indians who show the Pilgrims how to add a fish to the hole when seed is planted. This was composting basically after hole. In its current form, it only involves digging a hole (about 12 inches deep) into your garden area using a post hole digger, inserting your waste and then replenishing the hole with the soil removed. - once you have collected enough waste, you dig and 'plant' a new hole. This method could begin to feed surrounding plants as they break down. It takes about the same amount of time to complete this compostage process as with the trench method.

Composting does not need to be time-consuming or labor intensive. It will start you on the way to a greener lifestyle and a smaller carbon footprint by incorporating any of these passive composting methods.

IMPROVE YOUR GARDEN SOIL (AND REDUCE WASTE)

Soils in areas which were never worked before rarely have the qualities necessary to grow domesticated plants and vegetables. While soil may be covered in grasses and other naturally occurring flora in a particular area, modern plant breeds have been selected over the years for the varieties producing the highest yields. Only when rooted in a soil that meets those conditions can these plants fulfill their potential. The best soils for gardening are generally loose and friable (also referred to as tilth), spring back when compacted and even when wet, easily absorb water, retain the water until required, contain nutrients necessary for plant development , support a thriving population of beneficial organisms, have good pH buffering capabilities, and are resistant to erosion. The best way to improve soil conditions for gardening is by introducing "soil modifications." Soil modifications are anything that changes soil characteristics. Some soil modifications improve the characteristics of soils better than others. For example , adding clay to sandy soil or sand to clay like soils once was common practice and this improved soil tilth for a couple of years. However, the soil would often become as hard as concrete after a few years as the particles of different sizes compacted themselves into a tight matrix.

That was the opposite of the desired effect so clearly this method of soil modification is not ideal. Compost is one of the best soil modifications and it also happens to be one that all gardeners can access. This is because a gardener can either buy compost, or even his own compost in "grow." A certain percentage of a garden for the sole purpose of enriching the soil should be planted each year. A large portion of the garden area could be devoted to growing plants in areas with very poor soils during the first year, which will produce lots of good quality compost that will speed the process of soil improvement along. Certain of the best plants are legumes for this purpose. One of the beautiful things about composting with worms is that the composting process can be completed in a shorter amount of time than without worms once a large population of worms has been established. Worm compost is also more pound efficient for pound than most other compost. That means less shoveling for the gardener, and less work.

A good composting bin needs to be installed first. Worms aren't picky on what is going to work with so many different ways that they live. Everything was used, from stacked car tires to old refrigerators. To red wigglers, the most important thing is that sufficient ventilation is given and the temperature does not exceed extreme, under freezing and above 105 degrees is to extreme.

When you pick a home you need to install "bedding" for the worms.

What's Sleeping? Bedding is the material inside which the worms live.

I.   Blank paper

II.   Cardboard scrapped

III.   Peat moose

IV.   Leaves Dead

V.   Ancient Manure

VI.   Aged manure (fresh manure not used for bedding)

VII.   Coat coir

Dirt / Yard soil is NOT bedding. Adding a little is perfect but little more than a handful. The combination of different styles of bedding is good and perfect

The bedding will be warm. Get a container and bring in some water. Then take a handful of your bedding, put it in the water and let it soak for a few seconds. And suck out the excess water much as a sponge was being squeezed out. That is all it takes to humidify the bedding. Take that handful of humid bedding now and place it in the bottom of the worm bin. Repeat this until you've got about 4 inches of bedding underneath. Now you're done with bedding.

Just an interesting note here is that worms can live alone in humid bedding. The problem is a lack of food so they wouldn't multiply or develop much overtime. Next move is to attach a small amount of food to the bedding by putting it on top. Tiny amount means a cup full.

What is gastronomy? Worms are not picky eaters so it should work with just about any fruit , vegetable, nut or bean. Coffee and filters, egg shells, pasta, and even meat and cheese are included. The trouble with meat and cheese is that if you want stinky worms, they will stink like crazy so don't add them to it. Cover this food with a bit of bedding to keep away flies and smells. You might add another or two layers of food, just don't get it so deep that air won't infiltrate to the bottom. It is also important that the food is in layers and not "stirred in." This is because worms need to be able to escape into a bedding area from the food zones or they won't live. Now you're done preparing home for the worm. Every worm inside will be comfortable and cozy.

Now just growing them on top of the bedding, to attach the worms. It may take them one or two days to move into their new house, because they need some time to adapt to the new conditions. Think of it as if you are getting fish for an aquarium, it's best to let them slowly adapt to the new conditions. They are to be moved into their new homes after two days. You should see some worms clustered around the food you've added in another day or two. This is a positive indication that all things are well.

Wait until most of the meal is gone until you add more. The worms should be able to consume food more easily, slowly. As the number of worms increases so does its composting potential in your landfill.

It will finally be time to harvest the worm castings but it may take a while before the first harvest. The bin is only fed on one side in preparation for first harvest. Eventually most of the worms will migrate to that side over the course of a few weeks. Then there will be relatively few worms on the side that was not fed recently and the compost can be used in the garden.

Composting Benefits for the Environment

Aerobic composting is a very simple way to produce an unbelievably dense organic and natural material using a natural method called "aerobic decomposition." Composting refers, in simple terms, to the slow and continuous cycle of decay of various natural and organic materials, such as garden and grass clippings, very small twigs and sticks, tree leaves and other similar waste items, which occur every day in the natural world. Gardeners around the world know that compost is a superb soil conditioner and additive in the garden that improves the productivity and workability associated with almost every form of topsoil. Digging into your current garden soil in aerobic compost makes it richer and safer to help the plant life grow faster and stronger which will benefit our world in a wide range of simple ways from food production to irrigation as a side effect. This is precisely why gardeners around the world love and admire Aerobic Compost because it is full of mineral deposits and nutrients that are perfect for stimulating stable, lush, and rapid plant growth.

The technique behind aerobic composting depends on the basic idea of return, which works on what you put in the theory can help you determine what you get out of it. The most effective and also the easiest step you can take to reduce waste and grow a healthy, productive garden is probably the composting of backyard garden waste materials plus kitchen leftovers. Using compost in your back garden recycles vitamins and minerals as well as organic and natural material that helps to grow trouble-free flowers or vegetables using much less water, industrial fertilizers and even pesticides. Being aware of what compost is actually and how it can benefit your garden will result in high-quality compost even for those newbie gardeners, so a simple checklist explains the basic seven elements required to ensure an efficient and safe compost heap.

1. The Appropriate Types of Materials:- We are constantly told that we need a well-balanced diet for people to keep in good shape and exactly the same is true for the compost pile. None of the materials you add to your composting pile are the food and energy sources. Composting microbes best thrive on a mixture of succulent tasty nitrogen abundant materials known as "greens," such as fresh new lawn clippings, weeds, and even garden flora, as well as woody carbon rich elements known as "browns," such as autumn leaves, trees, straw or paper. I would imagine you've all heard before that it's a smart idea to put only food waste from the kitchen in your compost. Although this does work, a good balance of browns and greens is important for quick results to be achieved. You will fill your aerobic composting heap or composting bin with one part of "White" type materials to about 30 parts of "Brown" type materials as a general rule of thumb. This ratio is critical because an aerobic pile containing lots of browns will take a very long time to decline, whereas lots of greens will result in some sort of stinky algae mess. Keep in mind that all the materials you add to the compost pile will have these following characteristics,

too, making the best form of compost. 1), they must be bio-degradable, and 2), they should contain items that micro-organisms love. So that means you just need to steer clear of the stuff they don't like, such as assorted foods, bone fragments, fats and cooking oils as well as milk-related items simply because they don't decompose easily and usually make the compost heap smell terrible. Including meat related products in an aerobic compost heap is also much like giving rats and other such scavenging animals an open invitation to feed on your compost heap.

2. Product Size-Size really matters, as with a lot of things in this life. Adding large trees, large leafy materials or even whole food products to your compost heap will only delay the decomposition rate. All the composting microbes, bugs, and composting worms that live in your compost have only small jaws so they naturally like smaller portions to chew on. Cutting bigger organic food items into smaller pieces will help break down the bigger items into smaller bite-sized chunks by using a saw, garden shredder or the lawn mower. Nearly all bacteria and micro-organisms typically have a hard time finding their preferred food in large woody brown materials because of their rough coating and shredding the materials you add helps them on their way. Since the compostable materials are made much smaller, the microbes which perform the job of decomposition will be exposed to much more surface and inner area. When these materials are removed and reduced in advance,

this will help facilitate the process of decomposition as the smaller the bits they will decompose the quicker they can. However in shredding woody materials there is also a down side to finely. Such smaller particles are likely to create a more compact aerobic compost heap that minimizes ventilation and air flow within the heap, which in turn may lead to an anaerobic condition due to insufficient oxygen, so the heap will need to be forked over more frequently.

3. The Compost Heaps Size:- The size of your composting heap often makes a huge difference for the final quality of the finished pile, not just the level of decomposition. A compost heap must typically be at most equivalent to approximately one cubic meter (3 x 3 x 3 feet) in volume as this makes it easier to manage. Therefore, smaller aerobic batteries tend to dry out easily requires regular watering, although commercially available composting batteries with solid sides plus a lid can help keep smaller batteries humid. Bigger aerobic composting batteries take up a lot of extra space and need to be forked over to allow more air into their middle.

4. Water Content:- The right amount of water is another important component with regard to rapid aerobic composting. Microbes reside in thin watery films that surround the compost pile elements, thus helping to keep the compost pile at all times damp. If your pile gets dried out, it's not possible for the bacterial microbes to work effectively so include some extra greens. If the pile gets too wet, the bacterial microbes will not be able to receive the amount of oxygen they want to breathe so

they will include some extra browns and fork over the pile to mix it into. It's quick to figure out if your compost pile contains the right amount of water (40-60 percent), just take a small handful of the compostable material and then squeeze it out. When water flows through the fingertips then the pile gets too wet. To be able to guarantee bacterial decomposition and growth, the compost needs to be a little moist, just like a damp cloth or sponge, ideally.

5. Aeration-Material compostage is certainly an aerobic process. To help create compost of the highest quality easily, it is essential to have plenty of fresh clean air to let the microbes and bugs that live and thrive inside it breathe. Forking over your compost once or even twice a week using a spade or pitchfork helps aerate the pile as well as putting the newly added fresher external materials in its middle and vice versa. The forking or turning system, including dry or coarse materials in the compost heap, will help to increase aeration, prevent the production of odor-causing bacteria, and also help to accelerate the aerobic composting cycle. This practice of periodically forking over compost to help speed up the process of decomposition of the piles is known as "aggressive composting." Simply turning and forking the pile allows excess water to escape and evaporate, while also providing fresh clean air to the pile.

6. Micro-organisms and bugs:- Without the presence of the microbes and bugs that do all the work, no aerobic composting heap worth its salt would be complete. It is

these tiny little air-breathing micro-organisms and their larger soil-loving cousins that are naturally found within the soil structure that will flourish in the humid and nutrient-rich environment you have created. For example, the smaller decomposters fungi and bacteria begin the process of decomposition while larger bugs like worms, beetles, millipedes and centipedes complete the period of decomposition. What's left behind is an improving medium for almost black humus soil. To be able to grow and increase efficiently, all these macro-organisms and micro-organisms need an energy source, such as the "browns," which provides them with a source of carbohydrate and the "greens" which give them a rich source of proteins. They also require oxygen and water to survive on top of these. Like humans, though, these bugs do enjoy it warm and comfortable, which means that your compostable materials can certainly become a finished compost much quicker during the summer months as the rays of the sun help warm things up compared to the colder winter months.

7. Don't hurry, be patient:- It takes time to recycle aerobics. The composting speed or rate depends on several factors as we have shown, such as the moisture content, aeration level, as well as the percentage of carbon to nitrogen, the actual ratio of greens to browns. Aeration and humidity are generally the two key factors that influence the amount of time needed to create your finished compost. So you can support Mother Nature on her way by forking and turning your compost heap regularly, which is likely to produce quality compost in the summer in about one to two months, while monthly

turns will produce compost from about four to six months in time. The speediest composting occurs when the brown and green materials have already been pre-mixed, adding some previous microbe-rich compost and turning or mixing the pile weekly, as well as controlling the air and water content. But if it's all too much effort then sit back, relax and let the bugs do the job. Aerobic compost is a excellent soil fertilizer in the garden that improves the garden soil's workability and effectiveness. The correct quantity and types of materials you add to the compost heap really make a huge difference on quality level and composting time. You should think of your aerobic compost heap as a self-contained eco-system, and in order to grow and maintain it, this specific eco-system needs the appropriate mixture of ingredients and materials such as "Oxygen" (air), "Warmth" (sun), "Meat" (compostable materials) and "Moisture" (water), resulting in the consistency and quantity of the finished compost. To learn more about how "Aerobic Composting" works, to obtain more knowledge about the different composting methods and materials available, or to explore the advantages and drawbacks of composting, read our composting article today and find out how composting helps to turn your waste into soil and also to learn more about the various ways you can grow good quality compost in your garden.

My Wriggly Friends Help Make Compost

Now let's turn over again to worm composting. I knew about composting. I have a small composting pile brewing in my backyard. However, the first time I've heard of worm composting, I had to ask (embarrassingly I might add) twice if the person was not joking. When I got home, I searched the web and found out that those wriggly friends do help make compost. The process is interestingly different from the regular composting procedure.

Work composting or vermiculture is easy, affordable, and low-maintenance way of creating compost. It has a lot of advantages. Definitely it requires less work, just let the worms eat up all your scraps and in two months you'll have rich compost at your disposal.

The worms used in composting are the brown-nose worms or redworms. (That's where the name of my website "RedWormFarms.com" comes from.) They work best in containers and on moistened bedding. Those night crawlers or large, soil-burrowing worms are not good for composting purposes. Just stick with the redworms and things will work out well. All you need to do is add food waste to the container and soon enough the worms will eat them up and convert compost together with the bedding.

Before placing your redworms inside containers, place a nice layer of paper to serve as bedding for the worms. Any kind of paper will do, but it has been observed that the worms will consume newspapers, cardboards, paper towels and other coarse papers faster. The worms will eat this layer of bedding together with the scraps of food to convert them in compost. You can also add a bit soil on top of the paper and a few pieces of leaves. If your redworm container is located outside the house, try considering adding livestock manure on it. Redworms love them.

Fruits, grain, or vegetables are great for worm composting. The redworms can even eat egg shells, coffee grounds, and even tea bags. Avoid giving them meat, fish, oil, and other animal products. Like the traditional composting, these materials only attract pests to the composting bin and also produce bad smell.

The proportion of worms to food scraps will be based on how much scrap you like to be composted in a week. For example, if you want 1 pound of food scrap to be composted a week, all you need is also a pound of redworms. You don't need to add redworms into the container unless you want to increase the amount of food scraps you intend to compost in a weekly basis.

For containers, keep it well ventilated to let the air in and let the excess moisture out. You can use plastic bins, and even wooden boxes for worm composting.

The time to harvest would be when the container is full. Scoop out the undigested food scraps as well as the works which are usually on the top few inches of the material. The remaining material inside the container is your compost. To remove the remaining worms from compost, you can spread the compost under the sunlight.

Leave a few small mounds of compost. As the heat dries the compost, the worms will gather in the mounds. Just be careful not to leave the compost under the sun that long or the worms will die.

Afterwards, you can place the worms in the container again and repeat the process all over. You see, this is how our wriggly friends help make compost and for those who don not mind the feeling of worms in their hands, this might be a good and easy way to make compost.

BONUS: HOW TO START WITH WORM COMPOSTING

The proverbial win-win situation is worm composting — also known as vermiculture —. Why?

- It gives you an easy way of disposing of organic waste, such as vegetable peelings.

- It saves landfill space in the county which is good for the environment.

- It provides worms with a happy home, and all the free "eats" they might want.

- The best of all: The homegrown compost is a great way to feed and nurture plants for those who have gardens or even potted plants.

Worm composting, dubbed "the organic garbage disposal" by some advocates, recycles food waste into a rich, dark, earth-smelling soil conditioner. It's such great stuff that Planet Natural offers a variety of organic compost ranging in price from $5.95 to $10.95 as well as compost-containing potting soils. And despite its reputation, worm composting needn't be a smelly effort. If you're careful about setting things upright, your compost bin shouldn't be stinky. Worm composting is increasingly seen as a way of helping our environment and reducing waste. Throughout California, the City of Oakland has a recycling program specifically for food waste. The City of Vancouver in British Columbia, Canada, provides people with worm bins and even has a hotline that you can call to find where to buy worms. Spokane, Washington posts information on how to get started in worm composting to encourage residents to try this eco-friendly garbage disposal.

You need: worms, a container, and a "bedding" to get started.

THE WORMS

Do not go out and dig out night-time crawlers who live by your home in the soil to populate your compost bin. Nightcrawlers must tunnel to eat and survive through dirt and cannot live on vegetable waste. Instead, red-worms are needed — Eisenia foetida (also known as red wiggler, brandling or manure worm), and Lumbricus rubellus (manure worm). You can buy worms from such places as my website RedWormFarms.com or other specialized sites. Sounds a bit strange but yes — it really works, you can order your worms online and they are sent to you by mail. If you have the time and access, you can also find a horse stable and recover worms from horse manure or ask a farmer to ransack his manure pile for worms.

For every pound of food waste per day, Mary Appelh author of "Worms Eat My Garbage" recommends two pounds of worms — about 2,000 wigglers —. (Some experts recommend a one-to-one ratio — one pound of worms per one pound of garbage.) To figure out how much food waste your household generates, monitor it for a week, and divide it by seven. When populating your bin with worms, also keep in mind that worms can double their populations every 90 days, provided you give them adequate food and a good home. It's probably best to start with slightly fewer worms than you need, and just expect your worm population to grow to meet your demand for organic waste processing.

THE COMPOST BIN

The worms will also need a jar. Here you will find on sale a variety of worm bins including the Wormtopia and the Can O Worms. They are reasonably priced at between USD 100 - 130. You could also create your own if you prefer. When it comes to compost size matters. You're going to want a container that's between 8 and 12 inches deep. Wood is a strong building material. If you don't feel like building from scratch, even a "Rubbermaid" type tub can be adapted and turned into a composting bin. Books like "Worms Eat My Garbage" give you details on how to construct your compost bin. Only note that worms like dark, moist (not wet) environments, and they dislike light. Any container should have an opaque character.

Bins can be found from under the sink outside the kitchen, or in your garage. Temperature is one important consideration. Ideally, a worm compost bin should be located in areas between 40 and 80 degrees Fahrenheit. Red worms generally prefer temperatures of between 55 and 77 degrees. If you live in a harsh winter climate, you'll need to push your bin inside during the winter months, or seasonally composting. Another consideration: worms are like humans because they don't like any noise or vibrations. Keep them away from areas of high traffic.

The Setup

You are ready to set up your "compost store" once you have the worms and the containers. First, you want to build your worms a home, and one that will make them happy and productive. You'll need bedding that fills the bin from a third to a half full. Soak up a large quantity of shredded newspapers or cardboard to make bedding. Worms want a 75 % water environment. Newspapers should take just a few minutes to take up enough water to make bedding properly. Allow the cardboard to soak overnight, such as rolls of toilet paper and tissue boxes. Do not use garden soil, or mix in the bedding fresh cow, horse, or chicken manure. These emit gases and will increase your compost bin's temperature. You could have your worms "cooked" to death. Once you have soaked the bedding matter, wring it out until it is moist, but not dripping. Place it with something gritty like a bit of soil, fine sand, leaves, cornstarch, sawdust, or ground eggshells into the bin. (Worms don't have teeth so they need something gritty to help them grind the paper and food.) Once your bin is up and running it will be self-sufficient so you won't need to add any additional grit before you collect the worm castings and clean the bin.

To make your worms feel at home, dig down and place your worms there until about the middle of the bedding. Don't just hang them up. Then put the lid on the bin, keeping it at a moderate temperature. Leave them to settle in alone for about a week. They are going to feed off the bedding.

FEEDING

Start feeding your worms with food scraps like fruit and vegetable peels, pulverized eggshells, tea bags, and coffee grounds after about a week. Avoid meat scraps, bones, fish, leftover dairy products, and oily foods as these will make your pile of compost smell and attract flies and rodents as well. Experts are divided on whether to toss pasta and grains into the compost or throw them away in regular garbage. Your best bet is experimenting and letting your worms tell you what they are going to eat or not eat.

There are certain things of course that worms won't eat or shouldn't eat. Do not dispose of glass, aluminum or plastic foil in your compost. While paper can be used as bedding, don't include colored printed paper on it. The worms are toxic to many colored inks. Eviting rubber bands and sponges too. It is best to feed the worms in small quantities once a week. You will end up with a stinking compost bin when you feed them more than they can handle as the garbage literally back up. Compost does not smell. The foul smell comes from the rotting food which the worms have not yet consumed. If you give them meals of an appropriate size — not supersized entries — they can eat the food before it begins to rot (and smell).

Chop up the vegetable matter if they eat too slowly, which is easier for them to eat and gives new meaning to the term "fast food." If the chopping doesn't help enough, reduce the amount of organic matter you're feeding. When feeding your worms, you can check and see how things are going. Give some extra paper bedding to soak up the excess, if the bedding is wet. (Remember the bedding should be wet, not dripping.) If the bedding is too cold, use spray bottle water to moist it. Once your compost bin is up and running it requires little maintenance until little or no original bedding is visible and the contents of the bin are reduced in bulk and consist mainly of brown and "earthy"-looking worm castings. Once your bin has reached that point it is time to harvest the worm castings and give new bedding to your worms. Between two and a half months to every six months, casts can be harvested anywhere, depending on how many worms you have and how much food you give them.

HARVESTING

There are many different methods of harvesting. For those with the time and patience or small children, you pour the contents of the bin onto a large plastic sheet and then separate the worms from the compost manually. Typically kids love to assist with collecting the worm castings. Remember your helpers should wear gloves as well as yourself. Once all the worm castings have been removed, keep some of the compost aside to mix in with the new bedding and then start the cycle all over again.

A more common way of harvesting is to push everything to one side of the bin - worms, castings, bedding, food. Partially pick up decomposed materials and move to the other side. Put some food over partially decomposed products. Replace the lid, and leave for a few weeks alone. The worms should migrate over into the new food during that time. Put on a pair of gloves once they have gone to the other side, and harvest the castings. Make sure no worms are removed in the process. Then give the worms new bedding with some leftover compost mixed in.

Compost is useful whether you have an apartment or a backyard garden adorned with potted plants. Use compost to enrich the potting soil and garden soil. It does a great mulch, too. It's relatively trouble-free and you're not just helping your plants but also the environment.

CONCLUSION

Have you ever had any very nice soil around your house to garden? Few are. The clay-like soil prevented good water drainage in my case, and was difficult to cultivate new plants. Many times the sand content was too high , causing the opposite problem-accumulation of water. Additionally, there was a lack of a proper soil nutrient for large plants. One could replace all the soil-a time consuming process that is very expensive, build raised beds or work to improve existing conditions. Composting is the answer for that. Composting is the decomposition of plant remains and other once-living materials to produce an earthy, dirty, crumbly layer that is ideal for adding or enriching garden soil to houseplants. Helping the environment is a great way to. Composting is the process by nature of recycling decomposed organic materials into a rich soil called compost.

Composting is much like cooking, and the easiest compost recipe requires blending parts of green or wet material, high in nitrogen and high in carbon, brown or dry matter. Home composting is both fun and simple to do, and does not require significant time, money and effort investments to be successful. Composting is a cheap, natural process that transforms the waste from your kitchen and garden into valuable food for your garden. Composting is a way of reducing the amount of agricultural waste and returning it to soil for the benefit of growing crops. You'll love your garden for it.